First World War
and Army of Occupation
War Diary
France, Belgium and Germany

47 DIVISION
Divisional Troops
239 Machine Gun Company
13 July 1917 - 31 October 1917

WO95/2721/2

The Naval & Military Press Ltd
www.nmarchive.com
Published in association with The National Archives

Published by

The Naval & Military Press Ltd

Unit 10 Ridgewood Industrial Park,

Uckfield, East Sussex,

TN22 5QE England

Tel: +44 (0) 1825 749494

www.naval-military-press.com

www.nmarchive.com

This diary has been reprinted in facsimile from the original. Any imperfections are inevitably reproduced and the quality may fall short of modern type and cartographic standards.

© **Crown Copyright**
Images reproduced by permission of The National Archives, London, England, 2015.

Contents

Document type	Place/Title	Date From	Date To
Heading	WO95/2721/2		
Heading	47 Div Troops 239 Machine Gun Coy 1917 Jly-1917 Oct To Mesopotamia 18 Ind Division 55 Bde		
War Diary	Grantham	13/07/1917	13/07/1917
War Diary	Southampton	13/07/1917	13/07/1917
War Diary	Havre	14/07/1917	16/07/1917
War Diary	Abeele	17/07/1917	17/07/1917
War Diary	Westoutre	18/07/1917	09/08/1917
War Diary	Le Poovre	10/08/1917	12/08/1917
War Diary	Fersinghem	13/08/1917	17/08/1917
War Diary	Busseboom	18/08/1917	30/09/1917
War Diary	St. Aubin	01/10/1917	14/10/1917
War Diary	At Sea	15/10/1917	31/10/1917

W095/272/1/2

47 DIV TROOPS

239 MACHINE GUN COY

1917 JLY — 1917 OCT

TO MESOPOTAMIA 18 IND DIVISION
55 BDE

Box 2721

Army Form C. 2118.

No. 239 Machine Gun Coy.

WAR DIARY
or
INTELLIGENCE SUMMARY.
(Erase heading not required.)

239 M.G. Coy Vol I

Place	Date	Hour	Summary of Events and Information	Remarks and references to Appendices
GRANTHAM.	13.7.17.	0450	Left for overseas. Strength:- 10 Officers 177 Other Ranks. 7 Horses. 47 Mules.	
SOUTHAMPTON	13.7.17.	18.00	Sailed for France on S.S. HUNTSCRAFT.	
HAVRE.	14.7.17	0800	Landed and marched to NO.1. REST CAMP.	
"	15.7.17		One Signaller admitted to Hospital	
"	16.7.17.		One Man admitted to Hospital	
"		1400.	Left Un Gare des MARCHANDISES for Concentration point	
ABEELE	17.7.17.	12.00.	Detrained and marched to 47th (LONDON) DIVISION at WESTOUTRE. Went to CURRAGH CAMP (huts).	
WESTOUTRE.	18.7.17.		Training in Camp.	
"	19.7.17		Training in Camp.	
"	20.7.17.		Inspection by G.O.C. 47th (LONDON) DIVISION.	
"	21.7.17.		Working party of 4 officers and fifty men carried up S.A.A. to Gun Emplacements of 142 M.G. Company	
"	22.7.17		Sun day. Church Parade in Camp. One Man admitted to Field Ambulance.	
"	23.7.17.		Training in Camp. One man admitted to Field Ambulance.	
"	24.7.17.		Move to BROKE CAMP. Company in bivouac.	
"	25.7.17.		Training in Camp. Two Officers and 138 Other ranks loaned for attachment to 142 M.G. Company during forth coming operations.	
"	26.7.17.		Training in Camp.	
"	27.7.17.		Training in Camp.	
"	28.7.17.		Training in Camp.	
"	29.7.17.		Party detailed on 25/7/17 joined 142 M.G. Company.	
"	30.7.17.		Training in Camp.	
"	31.7.17.		Training in Camp.	

R. Roberts Capt.,
Comdg. No. 239 Machine Gun Coy.

31 JUL 1917

Army Form C. 2118.

239th Machine Gun Company.
WAR DIARY
or
INTELLIGENCE SUMMARY.
(Erase heading not required.)

Vol 2

Place	Date	Hour	Summary of Events and Information	Remarks and references to Appendices
WESTOUTRE	1917 Aug. 1st		Company in bivouac at BROKE CAMP. Heavy rain all day. One O.R. to Hospital.	
"	2nd		Heavy rain all day.	
"	3rd		Two O.R. Killed, Two O.R. wounded, of party attached to 142 M.G. Company.	
"	4th		One O.R. to Hospital.	
"	4th		Rain most of the day. Company went for a short Route March.	
"	5th		Party attached to 142 M.G. Company returned. One Man of this party went to Hospital. Lieutenant J.C. DUNCAN reported wounded on 31.7.17, while with 142 M.G. Company. Instructions received to relieve party of 23rd DIVISION, in A.A. Defences at ABEELE. Sunday. Church Services.	
"	6th		Four Officers and 46 other ranks proceeded to ABEELE, to take over A.A. defences. Capt. H.J.S. DUNSMUIR was in charge of this party.	
"	7th		Training in Camp.	
"	8th		Instructions re Move of Division to Training Area received. Transport of Detachment at ABEELE proceeded to it. Remaining transport started by road for ST. OMER.	
"	9th		Company moved by rail from ABEELE Station to ST. OMER. Then marched	

Army Form C. 2118.

WAR DIARY
or
INTELLIGENCE SUMMARY.
(Erase heading not required.)

Instructions regarding War Diaries and Intelligence Summaries are contained in F. S. Regs., Part II. and the Staff Manual respectively. Title pages will be prepared in manuscript.

Place	Date	Hour	Summary of Events and Information	Remarks and references to Appendices
LE POUVRE	10th		to billets at LE POUVRE. (S. of ACQUIN). One other rank rejoined from Hospital.	
"	11th		Training.	
"	12th		Move to billets at FERSINGHEM. ordered. Three O.R. joined from Reinforcement Camp.	
"			Move to billets at FERSINGHEM carried out. Two other ranks admitted to Hospital.	
			Four O.R. joined from Reinforcement Camp	
FERSINGHEM.	13th		Training. 2nd Lieut. S.C. MOODY. joined the Company from 70 M.C. Company.	
			One O.R. to Hospital	
"	14th		Training. Three O.R. to Hospital.	
"	15th		Training. One O.R. to Hospital. One O.R. reported by O.C. detachment at ABEELE.	
			to Hospital on 13/8/14. Inspection of Transport by O.C. 47 DIV. TRAIN	
"	16th		Training. Range work. One Man returned from Hospital.	
"	17th		Sudden Move carried out by tactical train to II Corps Area. One Man rejoined	
			from Hospital	
BUSSEBOOM	18th		Orders received for two Sections to take over barrage positions	
"	19th		During night 18th-19th, two Sections took over barrage positions at I.12.B.14. under	
			orders of 141 Infantry Brigade. (Map Reference. HOOGE. 1:10,000 Edition 3)	

Army Form C. 2118.

WAR DIARY
or
INTELLIGENCE SUMMARY.
(Erase heading not required.)

Instructions regarding War Diaries and Intelligence Summaries are contained in F. S. Regs., Part II. and the Staff Manual respectively. Title pages will be prepared in manuscript.

Place	Date	Hour	Summary of Events and Information	Remarks and references to Appendices
BUSSEBOOM.	20th		Two section worked on BELLAWARDE RIDGE (J.7.a & c) during night 20th-21st preparing positions for barrage. Six O.R. wounded of which two remained at duty, and two subsequently returned from hospital.	
"	21st		Y day. Two sections proceeded to BELLAWARDE RIDGE for barrage on Z day.	
"	22nd		Z day. Company in four batteries of four guns each. Positions for two batteries in open shell holes, about J.7.c.5.6. & for other batteries in old enemy trench system at I.12.7.1.4. Positions were shelled at intervals during the night and day and on Y-Z night. The enemy sent over gas shells on two occasions. From 12 midnight 21st-22nd to 12 midnight 22nd-23rd. Nearly 150,000 rounds were fired by all four batteries. Total Casualties. O.R. Killed 3. Wounded 6. One Officer (2 Lieut. J.R.A. PRICE) admitted to hospital.	
"	23rd	11.30	Two batteries at J.7.c.5.6. withdrawn. Two O.R. to hospital (sick).	
"	24th		One O.R. wounded. One gun and tripod destroyed by shell fire. One O.R. to hospital (sick).	
"	25th		Situation Normal. Casualties Nil.	
"	26th		Situation Normal. Casualties Nil. One O.R. to hospital.	
"	27th		Casualties 4 O.R. killed. One battery from I.12.7.1.4. moved to J.1.c.1.8. to fire.	

WAR DIARY
or
INTELLIGENCE SUMMARY.

(Erase heading not required.)

Army Form C. 2118.

Place	Date	Hour	Summary of Events and Information	Remarks and references to Appendices
BUSSEBOOM.	28.		Special barrage to assist 15 Division on our left. 20,000 rounds were fired by this battery. There was great difficulty in keeping the guns going, owing to the wet state of the ground. There was only one dug-out for self filling. Inter company relief of two sections in the line carried out successfully. C.Q.M.S. killed and two other men wounded, bringing up rations. Two mules wounded.	
	29.		Situation normal. Casualties Nil. Positions for 4 batteries for barrage work reconnoitred at J.I.C. and work commenced at once. One O.R. to Hospital (Sick) One Officer 2/Lieut. W.L. Boyt, joined the Company.	
	30.		Situation normal. Casualties Nil. Any digging at J.I.C. almost impossible owing to the wet condition of the ground. One Mule wounded 28/8/17, died during night 29th - 30th.	
	31.		Situation normal. One O.R. killed. right 30. 31st. Work on barrage positions progressing well. Enemy Aeroplane flew over battery positions at 5.30 p.m. but was out of range.	

R. Ross Watt Capty
Comdg. No. 239 Machine Gun Coy.

Army Form C. 2118.

WAR DIARY
or
INTELLIGENCE SUMMARY.
(Erase heading not required.)

Place	Date 1917	Hour	Summary of Events and Information	Remarks and references to Appendices
BUSSEBOOM	SEPT. 1st		Two sections in barrage positions about 1.12.6.0.5 (REF. HOOGE 1/10,000) Situation normal. 15 O.R. reported from the base.	
"	2nd	7.30 p.m.	Relief carried out by 195 M.G. Coy. 1 O.R. reported from Hospital. No Casualties.	
"	3rd		The whole Company in Camp at G.22.6.7.7. (REF. BELGIUM. SHEET 28 N.W.) Training.	
"	4th		Training. One man rejoined from Hospital.	
"	5th		One man to Hospital. Training.	
"	6th		Two other ranks reported from Base. Training.	
"	7th		Seven O.R. reported from Base. One O.R. to Hospital. Training.	
"	8th	5.30 p.m.	Three sections relieved 195 Machine Gun Company in barrage positions at 1.12.6.0.5. (REF. HOOGE 1/10,000) No Casualties. Two O.R. reported from Hospital.	
"	9th		Sunday. Church services for men at Depot. Situation normal.	
"	10th		2nd Lieut. A.T. SINCLAIR and two O.R. killed. One O.R. wounded. One O.R. to Hospital. Barrage positions heavily shelled between 2.30 – 3.30 a.m. During night 9th – 10th. 24,000 rounds S.A.A. were fired in harassing the enemy. Three spare parts boxes destroyed by shell fire. 24 boxes S.A.A. taken up the line by pack animals. Situation normal. No Casualties. 6000 rounds S.A.A. fired from 2.30 – 3.30 a.m	
"	11th		24 boxes S.A.A. taken up the line by pack animals	

Army Form C. 2118.

WAR DIARY
or
INTELLIGENCE SUMMARY.
(Erase heading not required.)

Instructions regarding War Diaries and Intelligence Summaries are contained in F.S. Regs., Part II. and the Staff Manual respectively. Title pages will be prepared in manuscript.

Place	Date	Hour	Summary of Events and Information	Remarks and references to Appendices
BUSSEBOOM.	1917 Sept 12.		During night 11th/12th. Enemy shelled positions heavily with H.E. and Gas Shells. 6000 rounds were fired in harassing fire programme. Situation normal. 24 boxes S.A.A. taken up the line by Pack Animals. One driver wounded taking up rations. Two mules slightly wounded and limber damaged.	
"	13th.		Situation normal. 6000 rounds S.A.A. firing during night 12th - 13th. 24 boxes S.A.A. taken up the line by Pack Animals.	
"	14th.		One gun and tripod destroyed by shell fire during night 13th - 14th. 6000 rounds S.A.A. fired during night 13th - 14th. Casualties Nil. Situation normal. Two O.R. to Hospital.	
"	15th.		Situation normal. Casualties Nil. During night 14th - 15th. 6000 rounds fired. 8 Guns fired a special barrage at 4 P.M. to assist attack on strong post by party of Right Brigade. Numbers of rounds fired 30,000. 24 boxes S.A.A. taken up the line by Pack Animals. 1 O.R. to Hospital. 1 O.R. from Hospital. 1 O.R. reported from Base.	
"	16th.		Practice creeping barrage carried out by 12 guns. 1 Clinometer per gun being available no difficulty was experienced on working the left to time. 12,000 rounds fired. Relief carried out by 14th Aust. Machine Gun Coy. at 6.45 P.M. Guns and their equipment could not be got away owing to Heavy shelling of the YPRES - MENIN ROAD. 1 O.R. (C.Q.M.S) reported from 24th Machine Gun Coy.	2/Lt. H.S.FOWLER.

Army Form C. 2118.

S. Roland
Capt.
Comdg. No. 289 Machine Gun Coy.

WAR DIARY
or
INTELLIGENCE SUMMARY.
(Erase heading not required.)

Instructions regarding War Diaries and Intelligence Summaries are contained in F. S. Regs., Part II. and the Staff Manual respectively. Title pages will be prepared in manuscript.

Place	Date 1917	Hour	Summary of Events and Information	Remarks and references to Appendices
BUSSEBOOM	SEPT. 17th		Guns and equipment got out by limbers at 5 a.m. Preparation for move. 1 O.R. to Hospital.	
	18th		Move by road to GODEWAERSVELDE. Men comfortable in a barn. 3 O.R. reported from Base.	
	18th		1 O.R. returned from Hospital	
	19th		Training and Recreation. Two O.R. reported from the base.	
	20th		Training and Recreation. Two O.R. to Hospital.	
	21st		Training and Recreation. One O.R. rejoined from Hospital.	
	22nd		Move by rail to 1st Army Area. Company entrained at GODEWAERSVELDE. Train timed to leave at 10.55 p.m. but did not leave till 3.15 a.m. 23rd. 1 O.R. to Hospital.	
	23rd	9.30 a.m.	Arrived SAVY BERLETTE STATION. March to LES QUESNES. Comfortable billets.	
	24th		Move to AGNIERES. Billets very scattered.	
	25th		Training. 1 O.R. to Hospital.	
	26th		Move to ST. AUBIN. 1 O.R. to Hospital.	
	27th		Training	
	28th		Training. Orders to hold in readiness to proceed overseas received.	
	29th		Preparations for journey overseas. Inspection by Major General G.F. GORRINGE Commanding 47th (LONDON) Division, who in a short speech, expressed his pleasure at the behaviour and work of the Company, since joining the Division.	
	30th		Church Services for all denominations. 3 O.R. reported from 142 M.G. Coy.	

DUPLICATE 259 M.G.Coy.
OCTOBER

Army Form C.2118.

WAR DIARY
or
INTELLIGENCE SUMMARY.
(Erase heading not required.)

Instructions regarding War Diaries and Intelligence Summaries are contained in F. S. Regs., Part II. and the Staff Manual respectively. Title pages will be prepared in manuscript.

Place	Date	Hour	Summary of Events and Information	Remarks and references to Appendices
St. AUBIN	1/10/17	3 p.m.	Company entrained at MAROEUIL Junction for SOUTH.	
	2/10/17		In the train on the way to MARSEILLE	
	3/10/17	10 a.m.	Arrived at Marseille and marched to FOURNIER CAMP	
	4/10/17		Organisation for journey overseas. Drill etc.	
	5/10/17		Drill etc.	
	6/10/17			
	7/10/17			
	8/10/17			
	9/10/17			
	10/10/17		10 a.m. Coy. SR entrained on S.S. MINNEHINEE & took their Coy. transport in moving.	
	11/10/17		Remnant of Company embarked on S.S. MINNEHINEE. Transport embarked. Loading men & led horses into the hold, loose being the most difficult to get into the hold.	
	12/10/17		Horses aboard at dusk on the ship and in the water, for about 1½ hours before swimming.	
	13/10/17		S.S. MINNEHINEE — sailed for MALTA	
	14/10/17			

WAR DIARY
INTELLIGENCE SUMMARY

Place	Date	Hour	Summary of Events and Information	Remarks and references to Appendices
At Sea	Feb 15		At sea. The men were very crowded and the steamer had very bad and too weak to do in attending to the animals.	
	16	2 pm	Arrived St Paul's Bay, Malta. No one allowed to land.	
	17		At Malta.	
	18	4 pm	Sailed from Malta.	
	19		At Sea.	
	20			
	21			
	22	11.30 am	Arrived Port Said. Coaling took place, which made the whole ship very filthy, especially the horse decks.	
	23	11.30	Sailed from Port Said.	
	24	4 pm	Arrived Suez. Company went for a short march whilst we were at Port Said, the stopping of whipping machines having been obtained at Port Said. Animals groomed.	
	25		Suez. 1 O.R. admitted to Ship's hospital	
	26	12 noon	Left Suez	

Army Form C. 2118.

WAR DIARY
or
INTELLIGENCE SUMMARY.
(Erase heading not required.)

93

Place	Date	Hour	Summary of Events and Information	Remarks and references to Appendices
At Sea	Oct 27th		1 O.R. to Ship's Hospital	
"	28th		1 O.R. to do do	
"	29th		} At Sea	
"	30th			
"	31st			

A. Roolinh Capt.,
Comdg. No. 259 Machine Gun Coy.

www.ingramcontent.com/pod-product-compliance
Lightning Source LLC
Chambersburg PA
CBHW081617160426
43191CB00011B/2168